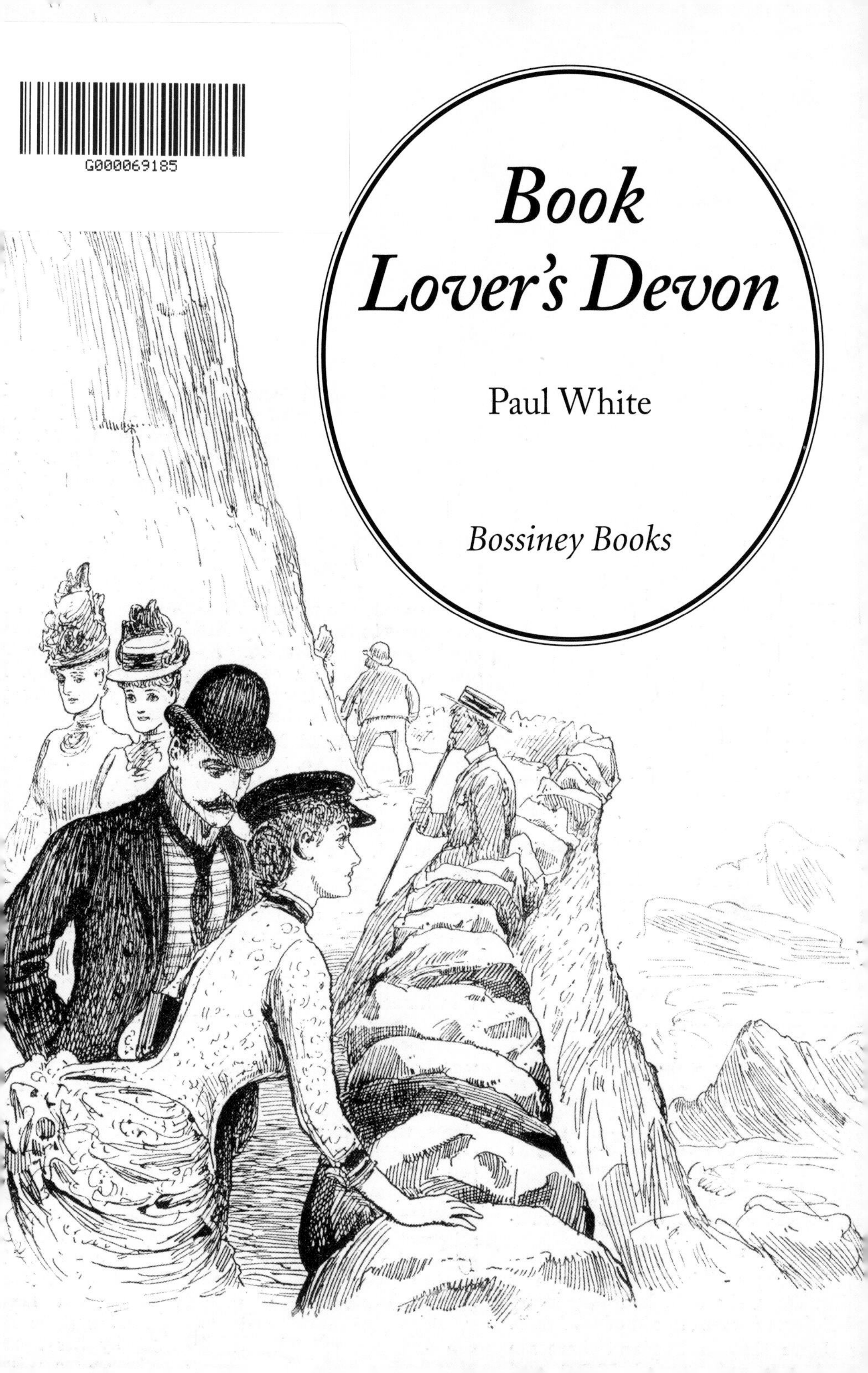

Book Lover's Devon

Paul White

Bossiney Books

Sir Walter Raleigh was a notable poet, among all his other accomplishments

The cover and title page artwork are from an illustration in the *Illustrated London News* (1888) by Henry Stephen ('Hal') Ludlow, 1861-1947

First published 2016
by Bossiney Books Ltd, 33 Queens Drive, Ilkley, LS29 9QW
www.bossineybooks.com

ISBN 978-1-906474-52-2

Printed in Great Britain by R Booth Ltd, Penryn, Cornwall

Introduction

Famous authors born in Devon have been relatively few, and often they have left Devon to establish themselves in the literary scene in London or elsewhere – for example Ford, Gay and Coleridge. Agatha Christie is exceptional in having returned to her Devon roots – after an exotic time in Mesopotamia. Many writers have, however, spent at least part of their formative years in Devon and it has influenced their work. Others deliberately moved to Devon later in life because it was a place where they could write in tranquillity, sometimes depicting the locality, sometimes not.

Many writers in the nineteenth century spent prolonged holidays in Devon, either for pleasure or for health reasons, and this is sometimes reflected in their writings – Jane Austen and Keats for example. Coastal resorts such as Sidmouth, Teignmouth and Dawlish became fashionable towards the end of the eighteenth century, but it was the arrival of the railways which suddenly made Devon accessible to the middle classes, and this undoubtedly had an effect on literature.

This book does not pretend to be encyclopaedic: among those I have omitted are local residents Mrs Bray, William Crossing (the Victorian Dartmoor authority), Cecil Day-Lewis (the poet laureate who wrote detective fiction as 'Nicholas Blake' and moved his family to Devon, but whose work and love affairs kept him in London), Rudyard Kipling who spent three years at Rock House in Torquay, Sean O'Casey who lived in Totnes from 1938 to 1964, and J D Salinger, who during WW2 worked for US counter-intelligence based in Tiverton. Famous visitors omitted include Fanny Burney, Elizabeth Barrett Browning and Evelyn Waugh who wrote *Brideshead Revisited* when on wartime leave at Easton Court Hotel near Chagford.

Nor can I pretend to have read all the works of every writer mentioned. Sometimes 'forgotten' novels are hard to find and, alas, sometimes once found they are hard to read. Fortunately many older works are available online, so these days we can at least get a taste before we buy the book.

The relative space devoted to different writers has depended on what I wanted to say about them, not about their significance or my view of their literary merits: do not imagine I am suggesting that Gissing or Gosse is more important than Sylvia Plath or Ted Hughes!

For space and other reasons, I have restricted myself to dead authors, but there are of course many writers living in Devon today, among them Michael Morpurgo, whose *War Horse* was inspired by conversations with veterans in his local pub in Iddesleigh, Hilary Mantel who moved to Budleigh Salterton in 2011, Michael Jecks who writes medieval murder mysteries located on Dartmoor, the children's novelist Philip Reeve and the poet Alice Oswald.

I hope that this book will interest you in its own right, but also that it will lead you to one or two authors you might otherwise never have heard of, as well as casting a different light on some you know well.

Jane Austen (1775-1817)

It is a truth universally acknowledged, that every location in a Jane Austen novel can be identified in the real world, and visited, and this certainly appears to be the case with *Sense and Sensibility,* where Mrs Dashwood and her daughters are obliged to move from their luxurious home in Sussex to a cottage 'within four miles northward of Exeter'. *Sense and Sensibility* was not written in one go. The first draft, written about 1795 before the author had visited Devon, was modified several times before finally being published in 1811.

It is possible to conclude from the descriptions in the novel that the action takes place in Upton Pyne, with the late 17th century country house Pynes featuring as 'Barton Park' and perhaps the farmhouse Woodrow Barton being 'Barton Cottage'. The Exe Valley is described – but it would probably be unproductive to look on the map for another mansion 'about a mile and a half from the cottage, along the narrow and winding valley of the Allenham, which issued from that of Barton [the Exe Valley]', and whilst 'the [marriage] took place in Barton church early in the autumn', it seems likely from the lack of any description of the church that Jane Austen had never visited it.

The truth about novelists' use of real places, like the truth of their portrayal of real people, is somewhat more complicated than is 'universally acknowledged'. It is easier to imagine events against a remembered background, and certainly easier to use elements of the real place when describing the fictional, but what has been observed will usually be modified.

It is known that Jane Austen visited Devon at least twice after her father's retirement, when the family were living in Bath and spent holi-

Sidmouth library and the York Hotel in 1829. Circulating libraries were a vital ingredient for a successful tourist resort

days at the seaside. In 1801 they stayed for more than three months in Sidmouth, at the suggestion of the vicar of Colyton, Rev Richard Buller. He had been a pupil of Jane's father, when his own father was bishop of Exeter. Sidmouth, according to Rev John Swete in 1795 was 'the gayest place of resort on the Devon coast, and every elegance, every luxury, every amusement is here to be met with – iced creams, milliners shops, cards, billiards, plays, circulating libraries, attract notice in every part.'

The following year the Austens stayed in Dawlish, a less fashionable resort at that time, catering mainly for invalids, though that would soon change. Perhaps they did not enjoy it, because they soon decamped to nearby Teignmouth, which was livelier and more fashionable. In 1803 they made the first of two visits to Lyme Regis, which is in Dorset but within walking distance of the Devon boundary.

Unfortunately no detailed evidence seems to survive of their exact movements – Jane's letters have been lost – but at Teignmouth they probably stayed on Den Promenade in lodgings called Great Bella Vista , a building which still survives though not with that name.

The majority of seasonal visitors would not have been from London or Bath, but rather from Exeter and elsewhere in Devon. The Austens doubtless became acquainted with them, and may well have been on visiting terms with Devon residents of the right sort, getting to know more of the scenery of south Devon.

In *Sense and Sensibility* the scenery of the Exe valley is described:

> The whole country about them abounded in beautiful walks. The high downs, which invited them from almost every window of the cottage to seek the exquisite enjoyment of air on their summits, were an happy alternative when the dirt of the valleys beneath shut up their superior beauties; and towards one of these hills did Marianne and Margaret one memorable morning direct their steps… They gaily ascended the downs, rejoicing in their own penetration at every glimpse of blue sky: and when they caught in their faces the animating gales of an high south-westerly wind, they pitied the fears which had prevented their mother and Elinor from sharing such delightful sensations.
>
> 'Is there a felicity in the world,' said Marianne, 'superior to this? Margaret, we will walk here at least two hours.'
>
> Margaret agreed, and they pursued their way against the wind, resisting it with laughing delight for about twenty minutes longer, when suddenly the clouds united over their heads, and a driving rain set full in their face.

Jane Austen took an interest and pleasure in the scenery of Devon, but there is no indication of any regional characteristics. This is because she concentrates on 'polite' society, a few of whom are a little unsophisticated, but no more so than her characters from other counties. There is no place for the lower orders, who might have had distinctive accents or attitudes: some writers might have presented bucolic yokels, but Jane Austen would have thought it wrong to mock the weak and defenceless: it was preferable to exclude them from the story entirely.

Sabine Baring-Gould (1834-1924)

Most people nowadays, at least outside Devon and Cornwall, have probably never heard of him, but he was in his time a prolific author on many subjects from folk-lore (*The Book of Were-Wolves*) to lives of the saints, from novels to books of travels. He was influential for

Devon culture in several respects but particularly for his collections of folk-songs (including 'Widdicombe Fair' – Uncle Tom Cobley and all) and for his contribution to early archaeology on Dartmoor.

He was the eldest child born into a gentry family who had been squires of Lewtrenchard (just south of the A30, between Okehampton and Launceston) since the early 17th century, and spent much of his childhood travelling in Europe, accompanied by private tutors. At Cambridge he decided to take holy orders despite his father's threat to disinherit him if he did so, and became a curate in Yorkshire, then rector of East Mersea in Essex. In his first post, as curate at Horbury Bridge in Yorkshire, he fell in love with the daughter of a mill hand: he arranged for her to spend two years in York learning appropriate manners, and then they married, when she was 18. They had 15 children.

Sabine inherited Lewtrenchard Manor in 1872, and this included the right to appoint a clergyman for the church, which meant he could appoint himself, henceforward becoming both squire and parson – 'squarson'. He promptly set about improving the church, for example by restoring the rood screen, and rebuilding the manor house. As a preacher he attracted a large congregation, and he composed a number of very popular hymns, including 'Onward Christian Soldiers'.

He regarded his folk-song collections as his most important work: *Songs and Ballads of the West* was published in 1889-91, and *English Folk Songs for Schools* was still in use when I was at primary school: I was a very unmusical child, so I shudder at the memory.

His *Book of Devon* and *Devonshire Characters and Strange Events* both make good reading. He was very aware of what was disappearing:

> The distinctive local peculiarities, the remarkable individualities of some of the villagers which have been, so to speak, my meat and drink as a novelist, are fast dying out. With free education and cheap railway travelling I doubt if anywhere they will outlive the next thirty years.

Many of his novels have a very distinct sense of places he had known: two are set among the Yorkshire mills, others in Cheshire, the Potteries and the Surrey heathland, and several in Devon, especially his beloved Dartmoor. In this sense of particular localities he was very like his near contemporary Thomas Hardy, except that alas he was not a novelist of the same calibre.

Richard Doddridge Blackmore (1825-1900)

RD Blackmore was the author of *Lorna Doone* (1869), which he did not think his best novel, but which is the only one to be remembered today. If you are an enthusiast, you can find his other West Country novels online in Project Gutenberg: *The Maid of Sker* (1872, set partly in South Wales, his mother's family home, and part in North Devon), *Christowell: a Dartmoor Tale* and *Perlycross, a tale of the Western hills* (1882, set in the Culm valley).

It is perhaps by a fluke that even *Lorna* is remembered, and certainly Blackmore suggested that was so. The manuscript was rejected by at least four major publishers, and when it finally came out as a 3-volume novel it was not a success, with 40% of the print run having to be sold off cheaply to Australia.

For some reason unknown, the publisher still went ahead with a single-volume edition – the equivalent of a cheap paperback following a well-reviewed hardback in later times. And at just the right moment it was announced that Queen Victoria's daughter was engaged to the Marquis of Lorne. Blackmore later joked that people bought his book by mistake, when they were really looking for a guide to what fashions would be in vogue at the wedding, but for whatever reason, *Lorna Doone* was suddenly the book of the season.

Blackmore's family were from Devon: his father was a curate in Berkshire at the time of his birth, but his mother soon died, and an aunt looked after him till he was seven. He spent much of his childhood in various parts of Devon, and was educated at Blundells School in Tiverton. Although he then lived elsewhere, at Oxford University, in London as an unsuccessful barrister, and then as a market gardener with eleven acres of orchard in Teddington (you will find Blackmores Grove and Doone Close immediately east of the station) he would say:

> In everything, except the accident of my birth, I am a Devonian; my ancestry were all Devonians; my sympathies and feelings are all Devonian.

His grandfather was rector of Oare from 1809, and then of Combe Martin also, and he had fond memories both of his grandfather and the landscape.

> Sometimes of a night, when the spirit of a dream slips away for a waltz with the shadow of a pen over dreary moors and

> dark waters, I behold an old man with a keen profile under a parson's shovel hat, riding a chestnut horse up the slopes of Exmoor, followed by his little grandson upon a shaggy and stoggy pony. In the hazy fields of lower hills some four or five miles behind them may be seen the ancient Parsonage, where the lawn is a russet sponge of moss and a stream trickles under the dining-room floor, and the pious rook, poised on the pulpit of his nest, reads a hoarse sermon to the chimney pots below.

'Stoggy' is a dialect word, akin to stocky. Blackmore assimilated the local dialects as well as the local scenery.

Lorna Doone was deliberately subtitled *A Romance of Exmoor* because Blackmore did not think of it as a 'historical' novel. He did not invent the Doones, nor the highwayman Tom Faggus. Both were local legends which had appeared in at least one book, but Blackmore successfully modified them to his needs – as he did the local landscapes. He explained:

> When I wrote Lorna Doone, the greatest effort of my imagination would have been to picture its success. If I had dreamed that it would have been more than a book of the moment, the description of scenery which I know as well as I know my garden would have been kept nearer to their fact. I romanced therein, not to mislead others, but solely for the uses of my story.

He was horrified that people should expect to identify the exact location of every single incident of his book, and then think him at fault when they could not, and it is rather ironic that his novel has become so identified with Exmoor tourism. On the other hand, without *Lorna Doone*, perhaps even those of us who have lived in the West Country might never have discovered the remote beauties of Malmsmead and 'the Doone valley'.

Sir Thomas Bodley (1544/5-1614)

Sir Thomas Bodley, founder of the Bodleian library in Oxford, was the son of a Protestant merchant, born at 229 High Street, Exeter. The family left England ten years later, to avoid persecution during Mary's reign, incidentally taking with them the boy Nicholas Hilliard, also born in Exeter, who would become a great miniaturist.

Sir Thomas on his return had an illustrious career, first within Oxford University, then as an ambassador to the Hague – a crucial post at that time, when Spain controlled Flanders. Yet his finest achievement was the refounding of the university library, and he also came to an arrangement with the Stationers' Company which was the beginning of the legal deposit system, whereby in return for copyright protection six UK and Irish libraries are presented with a free copy of every book published.

William Browne (1590-c.1645)

Born at Tavistock, educated at Exeter College Oxford, I think it would be fair to say he was a minor poet.

To England

Hail, thou my native soil! thou blessed plot
Whose equal all the world affordeth not!
Show me who can so many crystal rills,
Such sweet-clothed valleys or aspiring hills;
Such wood-ground, pastures, quarries, wealthy mines;
Such rocks in whom the diamond fairly shines;
And if the earth can show the like again,
Yet will she fail in her sea-ruling men.

Richard Carlile (1790-1843)

It is substantially to Richard Carlile we owe the freedom of our Press. He did not live to see it, but it was his determination and self-sacrifice which ultimately carried the day.

His father was an Ashburton shoemaker, who died when Richard was four years old. He received a free education at the Chapel in St Lawrence Lane till he was 12, then was apprenticed to a tinsmith. In 1813 he married and moved to London. When his children Richard and Alfred were baptised at St George Bloomsbury in 1816, he is recorded as a tin plate worker, living in Guildford Street, though when Thomas Paine Carlile was baptised at the same church four years later, Richard was a bookseller in Fleet Street.

It was in the economic crisis of 1816 that he began to take an interest in politics, and when put on short time by his employer, started a publishing business in the hope of making a living, printing Tom

Paine's *Rights of Man*, *The Age of Reason* and other radical books in pamphlet form, and hawking them round the streets for the poor.

He was present at 'Peterloo', and published his eyewitness account of that Manchester massacre – in a newspaper he provocatively entitled *The Republican*. He was immediately prosecuted for blasphemy (because of publishing Paine) and seditious libel – which was defined as provoking hatred or contempt of the government. At his trial he read the whole of *The Age of Reason* aloud, for two days, in the presence of the Archbishop of Canterbury: it was a clever device, since it was legal to print court proceedings and it had not previously been legal to print Paine's book. But he soon found himself in Dorchester Gaol for six years, fined £1500 and all his stock confiscated.

Whereupon his wife took up publication of *The Republican*, which began to outsell *The Times*, and was herself imprisoned, followed one after another by Carlile's sister and by eight loyal staff members. Carlile continued to edit the paper from within Dorchester Gaol.

Apart from proposing a republic, and a fairer economic system, Carlile suggested other appalling ideas, such as the abolition of child labour, equality of the sexes, birth control and sexual emancipation for women.

In 1899 his daughter Theophila Carlile Campbell wrote a biography, *The Battle of the Press*, in which she said:

> Before his six years of imprisonment had expired, Carlile was informed that it was Lord Castlereagh, the then Prime Minister, who was so determined to crush him, and also that it was his publication of the horrors of the Manchester massacre and his open letters to the King and Lord Sidmouth that gave the offence – Castlereagh himself having given the order for the massacre, and being solely responsible for it...
>
> He was warned by a faithful friend, previous to his sentence of imprisonment in 1830, that a measure had been discussed in the private councils of the Government, that the old law of flogging should be revived for his suppression, fines, confiscations, and imprisonments having failed to accomplish it. On hearing that the measure had been abandoned and a further imprisonment agreed upon, he 'confessed to having drawn a long breath'. He never despaired, however, but was always

> confident of success, and never had any misgiving as to the future outcome of the fight.

He pulled no punches: you will find him missing from most lists of famous Devonians.

Agatha Christie (1890-1976)

Dame Agatha Christie was born in Torquay as Agatha Mary Clarissa Miller. Her father was a wealthy American, whom Agatha herself described as 'a lazy man', who enjoyed his leisure and the company at his club. It was her much more decisive mother, Clara née Boehmer, who decided they should live in Torquay, and bought 'Ashfield', a large house with a garden of which Agatha had fond memories, but which was later demolished to build a block of flats.

Even if you are not normally a reader of detective stories, may I recommend Agatha Christie's *Autobiography* which is quite fascinating in its picture of her Torquay childhood – not that her childhood was entirely spent in Devon. She was often at her step-grandmother's house in Ealing (indeed a little known Agatha Christie mystery is that she appears twice in the 1911 Census, simultaneously at Ashfield and in Ealing) and also spent time in the south of France – which was an economy measure for the family at a time when the family fortune was declining: Ashfield could be let for the summer, and living expenses were far lower on the Continent than in England. In 1910 she and her widowed mother even spent time in Cairo.

In 1913 she met Archie Christie, who joined the Royal Flying Corps. They married on Christmas Eve 1914 and were then effectively separated till almost the end of the war.

Agatha worked as a volunteer nurse and then qualified as a dispenser in the temporary hospital in Torquay – which was the Town Hall, converted – where she learned a lot about poisons. It was that arcane knowledge which enabled her to write her first published novel, *The Mysterious Affair at Styles*, featuring Hercule Poirot: there was a large colony of Belgian refugees in Torquay at the time. Much of the the novel was written in an undisturbed fortnight spent at the Moorland Hotel at Haytor. The manuscript was rejected by several publishers before being accepted by the Bodley Head. It was of course the first of many crime novels, as well as the record-breaking play *The Mousetrap*.

So many of her novels have been dramatised as films or on TV, with

Poirot and Miss Marple becoming household names, that everyone knows of Agatha Christie, yet many people seem never to have actually read any of the novels themselves – which is a shame, because most of them are a very good read. (An exception is *Postern of Fate*, written when she was quite elderly and perhaps suffering from the early stages of dementia.)

Something over a dozen of the novels are located wholly or partly in Devon, with Torquay's Imperial Hotel and Burgh Island featuring more than once. Occasionally places appear under their own name, but for the most part they have pseudonyms, which has the advantage for an author that minor changes can be made to suit the plot – and that no local inhabitant can sue for defamation!

Indeed, one sometimes has the impression that known places are used like a chessboard, on which the characters can be moved around: the plot is what matters, and there is little time for description of scenery or atmosphere.

There are also subtle Devon associations to be looked out for, for example characters' names – Lucy Eylesbarrow, Lady Dittisham, PC Palk.

Agatha Christie's first marriage turned sour and ended in divorce in 1928. She then married Max Mallowan, later Sir Max, an archaeologist who frequently worked in the Middle East, and they bought the Greenway estate in 1938 as a summer residence. The house and gardens, overlooking the River Dart, are now owned by the National Trust, and are open to the public. Greenway features in the novels *Five Little Pigs*, *Towards Zero* and *Dead Man's Folly*.

Some other novels with Devon settings are:

The Sittaford Mystery
The Big Four
The ABC Murders
Ordeal by Innocence
Evil under the Sun
Why didn't they ask Evans?
Peril at End House
Sleeping Murder
And then there were none

as well as short stories such as *The Regatta Mystery* and *Double Sin*.

Samuel Taylor Coleridge (1772-1834)

This most famous of Devon poets was born at Ottery St Mary, where his father was vicar, and also headmaster of the Free Grammar School. Samuel was the youngest of 13 children. His father died when he was eight, and Coleridge was sent to Christ's Hospital school in London, and later to Jesus College, Cambridge.

He spent his school summer holidays at Ottery, and there are a few minor poems from that period, some addressed to local girls ('Songs of the Pixies' and 'To Miss Dashwood Bacon of Devonshire'), mostly rather derivative but sometimes witty, for example about a muddy road or the different standards of church music at Tiverton (good) and Ottery (very bad):

Plymtree Road

Th'indignant bard compos'd this furious ode,
As tir'd he dragg'd his way thro' Plymtree Road.
Crusted with filth and stuck in mire
Dull sounds the Bard's bemudded lyre,
Nathless Revenge and Ire the Poet goad
To pour his imprecations on the road…

Ode on the Ottery and Tiverton church music

… And oft where Otter sports his stream
I hear the banded offspring scream –
Thou – Goddess! Thou inspir'st each throat!
Tis thou who pour'st the screech owl note!
Transported hear'st thy children all
Scrape, and blow and squeek and squall –
And while old Otter's steeple rings
Clappest hoarse thy raven wings!

But these were all written before Coleridge met Wordsworth, who had an enormous influence on his style: alas, Coleridge became a much better poet after he had abandoned his Devon roots.

'Edmund Crispin'

This was the pen-name used by (Robert) Bruce Montgomery (1921-1978) for his witty detective novels, featuring Gervase Fen, an Oxford professor, the best known of which is *The Moving Toyshop*. Montgomery lived at Totnes, then from 1964 at Week near Dartington. His other career was as a writer of film scores, including several for the *Carry On* films and for *Doctor in the House*.

E M Delafield

This was the pen-name of Edmée Elizabeth Monica Dashwood (1890-1943), daughter of Count Henry Philip Ducarel de la Pasture, and a successful lady novelist, daughter of a diplomat. So 'EMD' was more than entitled to write the semi-autobiographical *Diary of a Provincial Lady*, which is the best remembered of her numerous novels – because it is one of the funniest books in the language.

EMD married Col. Arthur Paul Dashwood, of another aristocratic family, an engineer who had built the docks of Hong Kong harbour. After two years in Malaya, they returned to England and lived at Croyle House in Kentisbeare. EMD had two children and became President of the local Women's Institute, which along with a rather taciturn and boring husband sets the background for *The Diary*. But she also wrote more than 30 books, as well as magazine articles, and she would follow up her great success with *The Provincial Lady in America* (1934), *Straw without Bricks: I visit Soviet Russia* (1937) and *The Provincial Lady in Wartime* (1940).

It was her capacity to laugh quietly at herself, her circumstances and her own social class, as well as her tone of 'comic desperation', which made her a brilliant, and very English, writer.

Charles Dickens (1812-1870)

Dickens' most famous association with Devon is his renting Mile End Cottage in Alphington in 1839 for his parents, who stayed there 3½ years. John Dickens, the original of Mr Micawber, was hopelessly in debt, yet again, and Exeter in those pre-railway days seemed safely distant from the creditors. In the 1841 Census the enumerator recorded John Dickens' occupation as 'Charles Dickens' father', which was subsequently blotted out by a superior censor, but as John Dickens was by then writing begging letters to Charles' publishers, and even forging Charles' signature as guarantor of loans, the enumerator's description of his occupation seems highly appropriate.

There are, however, other Dickens connections with Devon.

Nicholas Nickleby opens in Dawlish, but there is so little local colour that probably Dickens had not at that point visited it.

Dickens' father-in-law George Hogarth had briefly, in 1831, been

A 'Punch' cartoon from 1852. Is there a private joke here? Did the cartoonist know about Disraeli's friendship with 80 year old Mrs Willyams of Torquay?

editor of an Exeter paper, the *Western Luminary*, and some say that Dickens first met Catherine Hogarth there, though it seems more likely that it was in London in 1834-5 when George Hogarth and Dickens were both working for the *Morning Chronicle*.

Charles probably first visited Exeter in 1835 as a political correspondent covering the general election for the *Chronicle*, an occasion when he formed a friendship with the local radical journalist Thomas Latimer – who later achieved fame exposing the corruption and nepotism of Bishop Philpotts. This was one of several elections Dickens covered, and doubtless it contributed towards the description of the Eatonswill election in *Pickwick Papers*.

On this 1835 occasion, Dickens stayed at the Turk's Head, where he encountered the original of the fat boy in *Pickwick*, and possibly also the original of Pecksniff – Samuel Carter Hall of Topsham, who later lived in Fulham. He also met Charles Kean (son of Edmund): when Dickens entered the ill-lit, ill-bolted Gents at the Turk's Head, the tragedian's voice boomed out, 'There is someone already here.'

None of which should make the slightest difference to your appreciation of the novels!

Benjamin Disraeli (1804-1881)

Most people are probably unaware that Disraeli was a writer as well as a politician, with his first novel published in 1826-7, his last in 1880. Some were written hurriedly to earn money, because he had made crazy speculations in South American mines, and was massively in debt, but *Sybil, or the Two Nations* is well worth reading. Although Disraeli was elected as a Tory MP in 1837, he was sympathetic to the Chartist movement. He later invented the term 'One-nation Tory'.

In 1839 he married a wealthy widow twelve years older than himself. Mary Anne Lewis née Evans (no relation to George Eliot!) apparently later said 'Dizzy married me for my money, but if he had the chance again, he'd marry me for love.' Mary Anne was the daughter of a Devon naval lieutenant, later a farmer, and was born at Brampford Speke.

They were a devoted couple, and she took to electioneering with enthusiasm, and was apparently especially popular with shopkeepers. Despite his continuing debt problems, Disraeli's London household in 1851 included six servants.

The couple, but more especially Dizzy, became very friendly with an eccentric elderly widow, Sarah Brydges Willyams, who had built a splendid villa at Mount Braddon, Torquay. She was a great admirer of Disraeli as a politician, and both were of Jewish descent but had converted, and both (probably wrongly) believed themselves connected with the same Spanish aristocratic family. They exchanged presents and voluminous correspondence and the Disraelis made annual visits to Mount Braddon. When Mrs Willyams died she left Disraeli £40,000 and her villa. She was buried at Disraeli's church at Hughenden, and both Benjamin and his wife were later buried in the same plot.

Torquay was not the same without Mrs Brydges Willyams: Disraeli sold the Mount Braddon villa two years later. He then became a very close friend of Queen Victoria, and was created Earl of Beaconsfield in 1876.

Sir Arthur Conan Doyle (1859-1930)

The Hound of the Baskervilles gives many people their first impression of Dartmoor, either from reading the book or in one of its numerous film or TV adaptations, yet it was written by a man who had only a limited acquaintance with the Moor – and the landscape is deliberately made scary to produce a classic gothic novel.

Doyle was born in Edinburgh, and qualified from the University of Edinburgh Medical School. When starting out on his medical career he accepted an invitation to work with a fellow graduate, George Turnavine Budd, who had set up a practice in Plymouth. The Budds lived at 6 Elliot Terrace, The Hoe, and Doyle joined them there. The practice itself was at 1 Durnford Street, Stonehouse. Budd came from a long line of Devon doctors. He was decidedly unorthodox in his methods, both medical and financial, and his plan was to give free consultations but charge for the medications. Needless to say, he prescribed 'in a heroic and indiscriminate manner'. After a few weeks they had a disagreement and Doyle left to pursue his career in Portsmouth.

Later in that summer of 1882, he took a short holiday with friends: they walked from Plymouth to Tavistock where the trip was abandoned because of foul weather, but the wildness of the moor had an immediate effect on Doyle. Nearly twenty years later, on a ship returning from South Africa, he met the war correspondent Bertram Fletcher Robinson, whose family home was at Ipplepen near Newton Abbot. Robinson told Doyle legends of the Dartmoor hell hounds, including those associated with the wicked Squire Cabell whose tomb is to be found in the old churchyard at Buckfastleigh.

They planned to write a book together, and in 1901 made a research trip staying at the Duchy Hotel, Princetown, but in the end, although Doyle wrote to his mother that it was 'a highly dramatic idea which I owe to Robinson', he wrote *The Hound of the Baskervilles* on his own. It brought back Sherlock Holmes after an absence of eight years, and was an immediate success.

George Eliot (1819-1880)

'George Eliot' was the pen-name of Mary Ann (or more usually Marian) Evans. She said she used a masculine name in order to be taken seriously. She was indeed a very serious novelist, and she was also a very serious holidaymaker, which is where the Devon connection arises.

Her partner was George Henry Lewes, who was already married. Even if he'd been able to afford it, he was unable to divorce his wife because he had condoned her adultery – they had agreed to an 'open marriage' and she had four children fathered by Thornton Leigh Hunt, the first editor of *The Daily Telegraph*. So from 1854 Lewes and Marian lived together openly as man and wife. Victorian society, at all class levels, had some surprising features beneath its moralistic facade, but George and Marian stand out by their lack of hypocrisy – though she did change her name to Marian Evans Lewes, so perhaps there was some concession to propriety.

Lewes was a philosopher and literary critic, himself the illegitimate son of a poet. At the time his relationship with Marian Evans began, he was increasingly interested in science, particularly biology. He had no formal training but he believed in the scientific method, and in learning from observation. George Eliot's greatest novel, *Middlemarch*, has as one of its themes the nature of science and scientists, and that was surely inspired by her relationship with Lewes, and by the people with whom she came into contact as a result.

Inspired by *A Naturalist's Rambles on the Devonshire Coast* by Philip Henry Gosse (see page 25) Lewes and Marian visited Ilfracombe in 1856, and were delighted by what they found:

> Having deposited our luggage, and ordered our *thé dinatoire*, we set out in search of the sea, and were directed to the 'Tunnels' – three long passages cut in the rock. We passed through them all and came to the most striking bit of coast I had ever beheld – steep, precipitous rocks behind and on each side of us, and before us sharply cut fragments of dark rock jutting out of the sea for some distance beyond the land, for the tide was now approaching its height. We were in raptures with this first look, but could only stay long enough to pick up a few bits of coralline, which, novices as we were, we supposed to be polypes.

But before long she had finished the literary work she had brought with her, and 'I felt delightfully at liberty and determined to pay some attention to the sea-weeds which I had never seen in such beauty as at Ilfracombe.'

They had taken local advice, and the true seriousness of 'George

Eliot' emerges:

> There are tide pools to be seen almost at every other step on the littoral zone at Ilfracombe, and I shall never forget their appearance when we first arrived there. The *Corallina officinalis* was then in its greatest perfection, and with its purple pink fronds threw into relief the dark olive fronds of the Laminariae on the one side and the vivid green of the Ulva and Enteromorpha on the other...

In *The Journals of George Eliot* she also describes the picturesque aspects of the coast and the delights of inland walking. She was clearly fascinated by her holiday in Devon, but when she began to write novels their settings were either well known to her, or meticulously researched. She would have recognised that she did not understand Devon well enough to base a novel there.

Following their holidays, GH Lewes wrote *Seaside Studies at Ilfracombe, Tenby, the Isles of Scilly and Jersey.*

When Lewes died in 1878, Marian was devastated. In 1880 she married a man 20 years younger than herself, John Cross, whose mother had just died. On their honeymoon in Venice, Cross threw himself off a balcony into the Grand Canal. Six months later, Marian died. Sometimes truth is stranger than fiction.

John Ford (1586-c1639)

Whilst his own name is little known, many people remember the titles of two of his plays – *'Tis Pity She's a Whore* and (as co-author) *The Witch of Edmonton.*

He was baptised at Ilsington, on the southern edge of Dartmoor, on 12 April 1586, the second son of Thomas Ford, who owned the small manor of Bagtor, and Elizabeth née Popham, whose brother became Lord Chief Justice. Bagtor Manor House was remodelled in the early 18th century, though parts of the 16th century building survive, and it is now a B&B. The Fords were much involved in the tin industry of Dartmoor.

John Ford was entered at Exeter College Oxford in 1601, when he was 15 or perhaps 16, and the following year he was admitted to the Middle Temple. It was normal then for the sons of gentry to enter Oxbridge colleges at that age, perfect their Latin and Greek, and then move on to more useful studies at the Inns of Court, where in addition to the law (which many of them would administer in later life as magistrates) they might learn mathematics and surveying.

Ford is generally seen as the last of the Jacobean playwrights, those specialists in 'revenge tragedies' who followed Shakespeare, though *'Tis Pity* (1626), *The Lover's Melancholy* (1628), *The Broken Heart* (1629) and *Love's Sacrifice* (1633), his best plays, were all acted first in the reign of Charles I so were 'Caroline' rather than 'Jacobean'.

'Tis Pity She's a Whore is a powerful if rather melodramatic tale of incestuous love between brother and sister (they were Italian nobles, which of course explained everything), a love initially fulfilled and then frustrated, in a play full of extraordinary violence and passion which annuls any sense of morality. Ford wants us to sympathise with the lovers, but especially with the woman. She finds herself pregnant and for the sake of appearances has to marry a man she does not love – but her brother cannot accept this. He murders his sister and arrives at a banquet with her heart on his dagger.

Similar horrors and taboo subjects, often involving compassion for a woman cruelly treated by the masculine world, occur in his other plays. Ford himself may have suffered from some psychological illness: as a wit subsequently put it:

> Deep in a dump alone John Ford was gat,
> With folded arms and melancholy hat.

Virtually nothing is known of Ford's life, and he seems to disappear from London around 1639, when it is assumed he died – but there is no evidence for his death. In fact there is a tradition that he returned to Devon, married and had children, but again there is no evidence to back it up. In several local parishes children of a John Ford were baptised, but there is no certainty that any of these John Fords was the dramatist.

John Galsworthy (1867-1933)

The novelist and playwright John Galsworthy, best known now for 'The Forsyte Saga' trilogy, developed a fascination with his family's Devon roots, and to some extent the (Dorset) Forsytes are a reflection of his own family's (Devon) history. His grandfather had left for London in the 1830s, but they had farmed at or near Wembury for centuries, and had probably come originally from a manor called Galsworthy in the parish of Buckland Brewer, near Bideford.

Galsworthy always felt at home in Devon, and in 1903 he stayed overnight at a farmhouse in Manaton called Wingstone. At the time he was having an affair with the wife of his cousin; she was named Ada Nemesis Pearson Goldsworthy, and they stayed at Wingstone several times.

After her divorce and their marriage, they took a long-term lease on part of the house as a summer residence, with the farmer continuing to live in the rest of the property. There was no electricity, and not even a bathroom. In their Kensington home they had two live-in servants, but not here. Galsworthy loved it and found it the perfect place to write, Ada Nemesis hated it and was bored stiff, with only the housework to keep her amused.

John Gay (1685-1732)

John Gay is another Devon writer whose name is less known than that of his most famous work, *The Beggar's Opera*. He was born in Barnstaple and educated at the Grammar School there. When his parents both died, he was apprenticed to a London silk mercer but was unhappy there and returned to Barnstaple. Later he went back to London, established friendships with Alexander Pope, Jonathan Swift and Dr John Arbuthnot and became a member of the Scriblerus Club. He sought hard for patrons, either politicians or royalty, and was not unsuccessful.

Most of his work is satirical, often burlesque imitations, which it is hard for the modern reader to appreciate without (which is unlikely) having some knowledge of the work lampooned, for example:

> Lo, I who
> erst beneath a tree
> Sung Bumkinet and Bowzybee,
> And Blouzelind and Marian bright,
> In apron blue or apron white,
> Now write my sonnets in a book,
> For my good lord of Bolingbroke.

Even his serious verse, such as the following tribute to Codden Hill south of Barnstaple, perhaps leaves us less than impressed:

> But the hill of all hills most pleasing to me,
> Is famed COTTON, the pride of North Devon;

When its summit I climb, O, I then seem to be
Just as if I approached nearer Heaven!
When with troubles depress'd, to this hill I repair,
My spirits then instantly rally:
It was near this bless'd spot I first drew vital air,
So – a hill I prefer to a valley.

Gay's greatest success was the *Beggar's Opera*, staged in 1728 by the theatre manager John Rich, which was said to have made Rich gay and Gay rich. Its leading characters Peacham and Macheath were on the one hand representations of two famous criminals, but at the same time Macheath was seen to represent the powerful government minister Robert Walpole, and the opera satirised the corruption of the ruling class. A sequel, *Polly*, was banned by the Lord Chamberlain as a stage performance, but the resultant publicity meant its publication as a book was immensely successful.

When Gay died in 1732 he was buried in Poets' Corner, Westminster Abbey, with an epitaph by Pope, followed by an epitaph Gay had composed for himself:

Life is a jest and all things show it.
I thought so once, and now I know it.

George Gissing (1857-1903)

Gissing is best remembered for his novel *New Grub Street*. He was born in Wakefield, earned a scholarship to what would later be Manchester University, was thrown out for theft, travelled to America, returned to London, and tried to make a living as a writer. His books suggest he lived in abject poverty, but this may be an exaggeration, if only a slight one. In 1891 he moved to Exeter and wrote three novels there.

Gissing made two unwise marriages, both to uneducated working class girls who subsequently had problems, the first becoming an alcoholic, and the second being admitted, five years after the break-up of the marriage, to an asylum in London's East End. Given Gissing's strange personality, and his dismissive attitude to his wives, it could be that their problems stemmed from him! Subsequently he seems to have found happiness with a French woman who wanted to translate *New Grub Street*, with whom presumably for the first time he was able to talk on an equal intellectual and educational level.

When he moved to Exeter with his second wife, it was to an unfurnished upstairs flat at 24 Prospect Row, where they shared a kitchen with a couple named Rockett. Predictably it was a disaster, and the Gissings moved to a flat in St Leonards Terrace, but while George loved the surrounding countryside he missed the British Museum and the buzz of London's teeming crowds, so they moved to suburban Brixton two years later.

In 1903 he published *The Private Papers of Henry Ryecroft*, which purports to be a fiction but appears to be a largely autobiographical work, supposedly composed of jottings found after the death of an unmarried hack writer aged 53 who had inherited a modest annuity and retired from writing – and from the world. Gissing explains in an introduction:

> He quitted the London suburb where of late he had been living, and, turning to the part of England which he loved best, he presently established himself in a cottage near Exeter, where, with a rustic housekeeper to look after him, he was soon thoroughly at home. Now and then some friend went down into Devon to see him; those who had that pleasure will not forget the plain little house amid its half-wild garden, the cosy book-room with its fine view across the valley of the Exe to Haldon, the host's cordial, gleeful hospitality, rambles with him in lanes and meadows, long talks amid the stillness of the rural night.

The book consists of Ryecroft's musings and essays on many subjects, with no plot, but is surprisingly interesting, though many of his attitudes (Ryecroft's, but Gissing's too?) are hard to take seriously – they would have been decidedly old-fashioned even at the time of publication. The title could quite reasonably have been *The Bibliophile*, since Ryecroft, in his earlier impoverished state would spend his last sixpence on a book rather than a meal, and his great delight now is being able to buy books. He is totally cynical about freelance writing as a career.

Unlike the real-life Gissing, who was an unsociable man but suffered from loneliness – a decidedly awkward combination – Ryecroft is utterly content with his life as a bookish hermit and, because the book is notionally a fiction, Gissing can perhaps express his own thoughts more openly than in any other form:

> These villages, how delightful are their names to my ear! I find myself reading with interest all the local news in the Exeter paper. Not that I care about the people; with barely one or two exceptions, the people are nothing to me, and the less I see of them the better I am pleased. But the places grow ever more dear to me. I like to know of anything that has happened at Heavitree, or Brampford Speke, or Newton St. Cyres. I begin to pride myself on knowing every road and lane, every bridle path and foot-way for miles about. I like to learn the names of farms and of fields. And all this because here is my abiding place, because I am home for ever...

As for his housekeeper, she is a great improvement on Gosse's wives!

> This poor woman who labours for me in my house is even such a one. From the first I thought her an unusually good servant; after three years of acquaintance, I find her one of the few women I have known who merit the term of excellent. She can read and write—that is all. More instruction would, I am sure, have harmed her, for it would have confused her natural motives, without supplying any clear ray of mental guidance. She is fulfilling the offices for which she was born, and that with a grace of contentment, a joy of conscientiousness, which puts her high among civilized beings.

The Private Papers of Henry Ryecroft received considerable critical acclaim. However, just as sales were beginning to take off, Gissing died, aged 46. His career had been a disappointment to him. He had never been able to make a good living from it, unlike his friend HG Wells, and success came just too late.

Edmund Gosse (1849-1928) and Philip Henry Gosse (1810-1888) – son and father

Edmund Gosse was regarded in his own time as *the* Great Man of English Letters but is now almost totally forgotten, apart from one masterpiece, *Father and Son*, which is an autobiographical account of his childhood in St Marychurch, Torquay, and his relationship with his father, (Philip) Henry Gosse, a man who lived two centuries after his time – he was a seventeenth century Puritan born in 1810.

Philip Henry Gosse was a significant author in his own right, popularising the active study of natural history. What he excelled at was field observing, especially on the seashore. Gosse virtually invented the seawater 'aquatic vivarium', and he certainly invented the name 'aquarium' for it, in *The Aquarium: an Unveiling of the Wonders of the Deep Sea*.

Alongside his scientific observation and categorising, Philip Henry Gosse believed literally in the Bible, and especially in the Creation. Even before Darwin's *On the Origin of Species* this caused him some intellectual problems, particularly with geology, where it was increasingly obvious that the evidence in the rocks showed developments over a vast period of time.

Gosse came up with an ingenious theory which he published under the title of *Omphalos*, Greek for navel. Just as Adam, when God created him, had a navel despite never having had an umbilical cord, so God created the rocks containing the appearance of a past history.

> My father, and my father alone, possessed the secret of the enigma; he alone held the key which could smoothly open the lock of geological mystery. He offered it, with a glowing gesture, to atheists and Christians alike. This was to be the universal panacea; this the system of intellectual therapeutics which could not but heal all the maladies of the age. But, alas! atheists and Christians alike looked at it, and laughed, and threw it away... He could not recover from amazement at having offended everybody by an enterprise which had been undertaken in the cause of universal reconciliation.

After this disastrous venture (*Omphalos* was pulped) Gosse returned to what he did best, such as detailed studies, including superb illustrations, of sea anemones and the genitalia of butterflies.

In 1848 Philip Henry had married Emily Bowes, both being members of a strict puritanical sect, the Plymouth Brethren. She was already 41 on marriage, and Edmund Gosse was their only child. His was a very strange and lonely childhood, with his parents devotedly dedicating their child to the service of God. They believed that a few souls were The Elect. Everyone else would go to Hell and Judgement Day would come in their lifetime.

> So confident were they of the reality of their intercourse with

> God, that they asked for no other guide. They recognized no spiritual authority among men, they subjected themselves to no priest or minister, they troubled their consciences about no current manifestation of 'religious opinion'. They lived in an intellectual cell, bounded at its sides by the walls of their own house, but open above to the very heart of the uttermost heavens.

When Edmund was seven, his mother was diagnosed with breast cancer and he was a close observer of her suffering, alone in lodgings with her so that she could be near her favoured quack, while her husband had to continue working:

> Language cannot utter what they suffered, but there was no rebellion, no repining; in their case even an atheist might admit that the overpowering miracle of grace was mightily efficient.

Emily died in 1857, and father and son moved to St Marychurch, where they had previously spent long holidays. To the father the place was just 'Marychurch': he would not deign to say 'Saint'. He promptly took over spiritual leadership of a small group of Brethren. *Father and Son* gives fascinating insights into both the sect and the family relationships, which could be surprising:

> Sometimes in the course of this winter, my Father and I had long cosy talks together over the fire. Our favourite subject was murders. I wonder whether little boys of eight, soon to go upstairs alone at night, often discuss violent crime with a widower-papa? The practice, I cannot help thinking, is unusual; it was, however, consecutive with us. We tried other secular subjects, but we were sure to come around at last to 'what do you suppose they really did with the body?' I was told, a thrilled listener, the adventure of Mrs Manning, who killed a gentleman on the stairs and buried him in quick-lime in the back-kitchen, and it was at this time that I learned the useful historical fact, which abides with me after half a century, that Mrs Manning was hanged in black satin, which thereupon went wholly out of fashion in England.

(It is amusing to remember that some of Agatha Christie's novels were set in St Marychurch, and that the village may have been one of the inspirations for St Mary Mead.) These conversations were a temporary relief from religious exhortation. Matters were greatly helped when Philip Henry remarried: Edmund's new mamma was only a Quaker, so whilst she was criticised by some Brethren for over-ornate dressing, life for the boy improved.

Although I had, long ago, read *Father and Son*, and have now re-read it with enthusiasm, I knew virtually nothing of Gosse's later career, and one of the great pleasures of my research has been the discovery of a splendid biography, *Edmund Gosse: a Literary Landscape* by Ann Thwaite (London 1984) which told me far more. In 1867, aged 17, Gosse became a Junior Assistant at the British Museum, then in 1875 he was given the job of Translator to the Board of Trade, in recognition of the large number of languages he could already read, and in 1904 he was suddenly offered the role of Librarian of the House of Lords – mainly to stop Edward VII putting his own nominee in the post.

But alongside all these jobs, Gosse was trying to become recognised as a poet and as a literary critic. He was a great seeker out of new talent, both in the UK and abroad. It was he who introduced Ibsen's work to England, and later that of André Gide and Yeats. He was an incredibly successful socialiser: he was acquainted with everyone of significance in literature over a period of sixty years – Tennyson, the Rossettis, Browning, Coventry Patmore, William Morris, Kipling, Beardsley, Leslie Stephen, H G Wells, Siegfried Sassoon, Robert Graves, the list is endless. And he had close personal friendships with Swinburne, Robert Louis Stevenson, Thomas Hardy and Henry James (with whom he corresponded for 50 years).

There were painters and sculptors too, and later in his life politicians (Asquith, Balfour, Haldane) and above all lords and ladies. Gosse was undoubtedly a social snob. But he was also a good friend most of the time, though there were many rows when he considered he'd been slighted.

Above all he was brilliantly sociable, an invaluable guest to have at your country house weekend, a mimic, an entertainer telling wonderful anecdotes, and yet at the same time a good listener.

For those on the outside of the literary circle, he became *the* person to consult about relative merit, such as who should be buried in Poets' Corner. He wrote literary entries for the *Encyclopedia Brittanica* and the

Dictionary of National Biography, and was on numerous committees such as the Royal Literary Fund. He was appointed as lecturer in English Literature at Cambridge, long before it became a Tripos subject – and his tenure of that post may have set that cause back, because in his lectures and in his writing he was famous for careless, unscholarly, inaccuracies. Every writer commits errors, which if we are lucky are picked up by publishers' editors, that endangered species, but Edmund Gosse committed many more errors than most – and at times suffered fiercely hostile reviews as a result.

However, that is not why he is now in the main forgotten. As a critic, he was accused in his own time of being 'a literary charlatan' – a label he himself subsequently used against several authors he didn't like, such as James Joyce. Perhaps by today's academic standards he was something of a dilettante – and he was certainly a populariser, who wanted people to enjoy literature passionately, as he himself did, rather than analyse it. In fact he was doing for literature – Nordic and French as well as English – what his father had once done for natural history. Popularisers are invaluable, but they write for their own time: they are inevitably soon outmoded and forgotten.

Gosse once said that Han Christian Andersen told him he wanted to be remembered for his novels, not his fairy tales. It is a common complaint of famous authors that they are famous for the wrong book – Blackmore for *Lorna Doone*, Williamson for *Tarka the Otter.* Gosse himself believed as a young man that he was going to emulate Keats: the general verdict on his poetry was that it was competent but lacking in revealed personal feeling. The reason *Father and Son* was and still is so successful is precisely that, for once, the real man is there to be seen: he is not hiding.

Thomas Hardy (1840-1928)

Hardy's Wessex is of course centred on his native Dorset, but Exonbury in 'Lower Wessex' (Exeter) features in a number of the novels. *The Romantic Adventures of a Milkmaid* is entirely set in Devon, with 'Silverthorne' probably based on Silverton in the Exe Valley (with the addition of some imaginary lime kilns), and the story 'For Conscience's Sake' in *Life's Little Ironies* is mostly set in 'Exonbury' – but there is far less feeling for an actual locality than when Hardy is dealing with Dorset or North Cornwall.

Robert Herrick (1591-1674)

Gather ye rosebuds while ye may,
Old Time is still a-flying;
And this same flower that smiles today,
Tomorrow will be dying.

Robert Herrick's most famous poem 'To the Virgins, to Make Much of Time', of which these are the opening lines, is a particularly lively version of the classical *carpe diem* poem, at which every seventeenth century poet tried their hand.

Herrick was a clergyman, appointed to be vicar of Dean Prior in 1629. He was bored in Devon, and spent a lot of time writing.

More discontents I never had
Since I was born, than here;
Where I have been, and still am, sad,
In this dull Devonshire.
Yet justly too I must confess,
I ne'er invented such
Ennobled numbers for the press,
Than where I loath'd so much.

The Commonwealth ejected him from his living in 1647, and he must have used his free time in London to good effect, because his great book of 1200 poems, *Hesperides*, was published the following year.

The first poem, 'The Argument of his Book', explains his themes – which it should be understood are very much those of Roman poets: Herrick's poems reveal little of himself.

I sing of brooks, of blossoms, birds, and bowers,
Of April, May, of June, and July flowers.
I sing of May-poles, hock-carts, wassails, wakes,
Of bridegrooms, brides, and of their bridal-cakes.
I write of youth, of love, and have access
By these to sing of cleanly wantonness.
I sing of dews, of rains, and piece by piece
Of balm, of oil, of spice, and ambergris.
I sing of Time's trans-shifting; and I write
How roses first came red, and lilies white.
I write of groves, of twilights, and I sing
The court of Mab, and of the fairy king.

I write of Hell; I sing (and ever shall)
Of Heaven, and hope to have it after all.

After the Restoration, Herrick successfully petitioned for the return of his vicarage, and died at the age of 83. Whilst he never married, he had a 'faithful housekeeper', Prudence Baldwin, who accompanied him when he was ejected, and was still living with him at the time of his death. Both are buried in unmarked graves in the churchyard at Dean Prior – right next to the A30, so today it's not the ideal place to contemplate rosebuds.

Ted Hughes (1930-1998)

Ted Hughes was a Yorkshireman, but moved to Devon in 1961 and spent most of the rest of his life in the county, partly at Court Green, North Tawton, partly at Moortown Farm near Winkleigh, the family home of his second wife Carol Orchard. His personal life was tragic, with both his first wife Sylvia Plath and then his partner, Assia Wevill, committing suicide. Read *Birthday Letters* and also his poem 'Last Letter', found and released in 2010 by his widow, and the reactions to it, if you want to know more.

Both Ted Hughes' poetry and his writing for children were much appreciated, and he was appointed Poet Laureate in 1984. There is a Ted Hughes Poetry Trail in Stover Country Park.

John Keats (1795-1821)

Keats was a Londoner, son of an ostler at an inn near Moorgate, but his mother's family was quite well off, and Keats would inherit a reasonable sum. He trained enthusiastically as a doctor but, having spent most of his money on that training, then decided he had no choice: he must be a poet. His work received a very mixed reception, some thinking him a genius, while a review in *Blackwood's Magazine* said:

The phrenzy of the Poems was bad enough in its way;
but it did not alarm us half so seriously as the calm,
settled, imperturbable drivelling idiocy of *Endymion*.

His connection with Devon was minimal, but *Endymion* was written in Teignmouth, where Keats stayed for seven weeks looking after his brother Tom, at 20 Northumberland Terrace. Tom was suffering from tuberculosis, from which he soon died and from which Keats himself would die a little over two years later. He seems to have arrived in Devon expecting a fantasy rural paradise, and within two days had written 'The Devon Maid', possibly before he'd walked out of the town.

> Where be ye going, you Devon maid?
> And what have ye there i' the basket?
> Ye tight little fairy, just fresh from the dairy,
> Will ye give me some cream if I ask it?
>
> I love your meads, and I love your flowers,
> And I love your junkets mainly,
> But 'hind the door, I love kissing more,
> O look not so disdainly!
>
> I love your hills, and I love your dales,
> And I love your flocks a-bleating;
> But O, on the heather to lie together,
> With both our hearts a-beating!
>
> I'll put your basket all safe in a nook,
> Your shawl I'll hang up on this willow,
> And we will sigh in the daisy's eye,
> And kiss on a grass-green pillow.

Charming. But can we forgive a man who slandered 'the abominable Devonshire weather... the truth is, it is a splashy, rainy, misty, snowy, foggy, haily, floody, muddy, slipshod county'?

Charles Kingsley (1819-1875)

Charles Kingsley was a very remarkable man, born at Holne on Dartmoor in 1819. His father was vicar there, then vicar of Clovelly and later (when Kingsley was already 18) rector of Chelsea: Kingsley remained passionate about Devon, though he spent most of his life as rector of Eversley in Hampshire. He said 'I feel myself a stranger and a sojourner in a foreign land the moment I get east of Taunton Dean.'

Both Kingsley's writing style, and above all his attitudes, have dated perhaps more than those of any other Victorian novelist, and one finds oneself at times admiring something he says, only to find in the next sentence some jaw-dropping example of jingoism, racism, anti-Catholicism or other bigotry.

In his childhood he saw the suffering of agricultural labourers and of Clovelly fishermen and their families, and his early novels

Yeast and *Alton Locke* show a sympathy with the Victorian working class.

Despite having severe religious doubts while at Cambridge, he opted for a career in the church. As a clergyman he was very active in his parish, and subsequently became an active campaigner nationally for better sanitation, drainage and water supply, especially for the urban working class. That, and a simple belief in God, would he felt deter them from revolution.

He is famous as a 'Christian Socialist' and as a tireless advocate of better living conditions for the working classes but, as fellow author Thomas Hughes wrote, 'he was by nature and education an aristocrat in the best sense of the word, believed that a landed aristocracy was a blessing to the country, and that no country would gain the highest liberty without such a class, holding its own position firmly, but in sympathy with the people.'

In 1855 he spent a summer at Torquay for the sake of his wife's health, and while there wrote *Glaucus, or the Wonders of the Shore,* a natural history book based on observation, and his fascination with sea life is a feature of his children's book *The Water Babies*, which is also in part a satire on the anti-Darwinists.

He publicly supported Charles Darwin on evolution – though a little further exploration shows his views might have been rather different from Darwin's: he can be found, a few months after publication of *On the Origin of Species*, referring to Irish peasants as white chimpanzees. 'To see white chimpanzees is dreadful; if they were black one would not feel it so much, but their skins, except where tanned by exposure, are as white as ours…'

At times Kingsley's Christian Socialism bore a disconcerting resemblance to National Socialism. Reading his books in the 21st century is often an uncomfortable experience. In his day his confident imperialism was well respected in government circles.

Kingsley was appointed as Regius Professor of Modern History at Cambridge, then private tutor to the Prince of Wales, and canon of Westminster Abbey. There is a prominent statue of him in Bideford, and of course a seaside resort was named after one of his novels: *Westward Ho!*

Christopher Robin Milne (1920-1996)

Christopher Milne was a charming man who founded the attractive and successful Harbour Bookshop in Dartmouth. He did not stock the *Pooh* books of his father A A Milne, and deeply resented their effect on his life, since from the very beginning of schooling his classmates had taunted him, and at Stowe School he had to learn to box to defend himself. His father realised early on what damage he had done, but by that time it was already too late. Later in life Christopher Robin seems to have adjusted, and wrote the first volume of his autobiographies, *Enchanted Places*, about his childhood.

Penguin Books

Penguin books is so much a part of our heritage that one might think it has always existed, but in fact the idea for it struck Allen Lane (1902-1970) when he was waiting for a train at Exeter in 1934, after meeting Agatha Christie. Paperbacks were not new, but Lane's idea was to produce them so cheaply that they could be sold as cheaply as cigarette packets from a platform vending machine, the 'Penguincubator'.

Allen Lane was born Allen Lane Williams, but the family changed its name to retain Bodley Head, the business co-founded by his uncle John Lane from Hartland, as a family business. There are monuments to the family in Hartland church. Allen Lane's daughter Clare is married to Michael Morpurgo, whose stepfather Jack Morpurgo was an editor at Penguin.

Eden Phillpotts (1862-1960)

What Hardy is to Dorset, Phillpotts is to Dartmoor. In an extraordinarily long career – his first novel was published in 1891, his last in 1959 – he wrote much fiction about his beloved Dartmoor and other parts of Devon, as well as poetry and plays. He also became President of the Dartmoor Preservation Association.

In contrast to Hardy, Phillpotts' work is largely forgotten, except by Dartmoor enthusiasts, and few of his books are in print. Is this neglect fair? Having read only *Children of the Mist*, and dipped into some of his other books, I don't feel able to pass judgement. Like many popular novelists of his day, he tends to emotional melodrama, and there are long poetic descriptions, but these are the result of close observation:

> Patches of mist all full of silver light moved like lonely living

> things on the face of the high Moor. Here they dispersed and scattered, here they approached and mingled together, here they stretched forth pearly fingers above the shining granite, and changed their shapes at the whim of every passing breeze; but the tendency of each shining, protean mass was to rise to the sun, and presently each valley and coomb lay clear, while the cool vapours wound in luminous and downy undulations along the highest points of the land before vanishing into air.

He was also a close observer of Dartmoor life, customs and attitudes. Direct speech in Dartmoor dialect is a major feature:

> 'An' what better word should 'e have?' piped Billy, who in the space of half a minute had ranged himself alongside his master. 'You to question the word o' Miller Lyddon, you crooked-hearted raven! Who was it spoke for 'e fifteen year ago an' got 'em to make 'e p'liceman 'cause you was tu big a fule to larn any other trade? Gert, thankless twoad! An' who was it let 'em keep the 'Green Man' awpen two nights in wan week arter closin' time, 'cause he wanted another drop hisself?'

Unlike Hardy, born 22 years earlier and the son of a stonemason, or DH Lawrence, born 23 years later and the son of a coal miner, Henry Eden Phillpotts was the son of a 'Captain on the Bengal Staff Corps, gentleman'; he was born in India and educated at a private school in Plymouth, so his understanding is that of a sympathetic observer and listener, rather than an insider.

Regardless of their purely literary merits, Phillpotts' novels are a wonderful evocation of Dartmoor's past, which in itself makes them well worth reading. It's a shame that they haven't yet been taken up as TV costume dramas, perhaps given the Poldark treatment.

Sylvia Plath (1932-1963)

The poet Sylvia Plath was married to Ted Hughes (see page 31) and they moved together to Court Green, North Tawton in Autumn 1961 and worked hard to make it their dream home. The following year, Hughes formed a relationship with another woman, Assia Wevill. Sylvia asked him to leave, and it was in North Tawton that she wrote most of the poems in her collection *Ariel*, before moving to London in December 1962 and committing suicide.

'Stymouth is a pretty little town, situated at the mouth of the river Pigsty, whose sluggish waters slide gently into a bay sheltered by high red headlands. The town itself seems to be sliding downhill in a basin of hills, all slipping seaward into Stymouth harbour, which is dammed back by quays and the outer breakwater.'

Beatrix Potter (1866-1943)

She was a frequent holiday visitor to Devon from her childhood, and the *The Tale of Little Pig Robinson* was set in Sidmouth ('Stymouth'), where there was once a herring fleet, but some of the illustrations originated in sketches of Teignmouth. Though published in 1930, it had probably been written and illustrated in the 1890s.

Beatrix's early experience of Torquay was rather unfortunate:

> I didn't much want to go. I did not take to what I had seen of Torquay… I sniffed my bedroom on arrival, and for a few hours felt a certain grim satisfaction where my forebodings were maintained, but it is possible to have too much Natural History in a bed. I did not undress after the first night, but I was obliged to lie on it because there were only two chairs and one of them was broken.

Sir Walter Raleigh (1554?-1618)

Every Elizabethan courtier tried their hand at poetry, but Raleigh was exceptionally good. 'The Nymph's reply to the Shepherd was his response to Christopher Marlowe's 'The Passionate Shepherd' – 'Come live with me and be my love'.

If all the world and love were young,
And truth in every shepherd's tongue,
These pretty pleasures might me move
To live with thee and be thy Love.

But Time drives flocks from field to fold;
When rivers rage and rocks grow cold;
And Philomel becometh dumb;
The rest complains of cares to come.

The flowers do fade, and wanton fields
To wayward Winter reckoning yields:
A honey tongue, a heart of gall,
Is fancy's spring, but sorrow's fall.

Thy gowns, thy shoes, thy beds of roses,
Thy cap, thy kirtle, and thy posies,
Soon break, soon wither – soon forgotten,
In folly ripe, in reason rotten...

But could youth last, and love still breed,
Had joys no date, nor age no need,
Then these delights my mind might move
To live with thee and be thy Love.

Raleigh was born at Hayes Barton, near Budleigh Salterton. His life is surely well enough known to need no description here.

William Makepeace Thackeray (1811-1863)

Thackeray was born in India, but was sent to England for his education. His mother and stepfather settled at Larkbeare near Ottery St Mary, and he spent some time there before going to Cambridge, and again in the vacations. Ottery features as 'Clavering' and Exeter as 'Chatteris' in his comic and satirical novel *Pendennis*, some aspects of which are based on Thackeray's own experience, but fall short of being totally autobiographical. There is quite a detailed description of the village.

Thackeray is less than kind about the inhabitants of 'Clavering St Mary', but perhaps they had reason to dislike the novel's hero:

> It was true that he gave himself airs to the Clavering folks. Naturally haughty and frank, their cackle and small talk and small dignities bored him, and he showed a contempt which he could not conceal...

The Exeter Subscription Library in Thackeray's day

And when Pen is found to have made a fool of himself, his family find the village folk have turned against them:

> Etc. etc. etc.: let the reader fill up these details according to his liking and experience of village scandal. They will suffice to show how it was that a good woman occupied solely in doing her duty to her neighbour and her children, and an honest, brave lad, impetuous, and full of good, and wishing well to every mortal alive found enemies and detractors amongst people to whom they were superior, and to whom they had never done anything like harm. The Clavering curs were yelping all round the house of Fairoaks, and delighted to pull Pen down.

But whether this reflects Thackeray's own experience of Devon, or is just a general prejudice against provincials from a London sophisticate whose default expression is a sneer, is impossible to say.

Anthony Trollope (1815-1882)

Trollope's novel *Rachel Ray* (1863) is set in Devon, in and around a town which can broadly be identified as Kingsbridge. Trollope was an incredibly well-travelled man, mainly as a result of his work as a senior civil servant in the Post Office, for which he made a number of foreign visits, for example to Egypt to improve arrangements for the mail to India and Australia, and to the West Indies to reorganise totally the systems there. His knowledge of Devon came largely from an early period in his career when he reorganised the postal services in Devon and Cornwall, riding on horseback 40 miles every day and ensuring that the postmen would have the most effective daily walking routes, none of which was to exceed 16 miles. He said he had probably gone past every house in the two counties.

Quite how a man who worked that hard and came near to holding the top job in the Post Office (but fell foul of the previous boss, Rowland Hill, just at the wrong moment) ever had the time and energy to write 47 novels, as well as numerous other books and short stories, who also wrote voluminously for the newspapers and magazines, and sat on numerous committees working for good causes, would be something of a mystery, except that in his *Autobiography* he revealed that he rose at 5am, started by looking for one hour at what he'd previously written, then wrote for two hours timing himself like a committed jogger – 250 words every 15 minutes. No robot could do better.

Rachel Ray is both a romance and satirically humorous at the expense of provincialism, and might as well have been set in Ireland, the Channel Islands, or one of the other English counties where Trollope had done the same job. The subject matter reflects his hatred of Low Church kill-joys, especially clergymen who weren't 'gentlemen' because they'd not been to Oxbridge, and his more general snobbishness about race and class. Personally I find his attitude to women extremely condescending even when at the same time he is pointing out sexist injustices in the Victorian social fabric: it spoils my personal appreciation of his novels, but that is a long-held view, and perhaps I am wrong.

Which could not be said by the hero of another Trollope novel set partially in Exeter, *He Knew He Was Right*. Louis Trevelyan, an unreasonably jealous man, expects total obedience from his wife, who unfortunately is in her own way equally bloody-minded. A sub-plot involves a Miss Stanbury, an elderly, rich and strong-willed spinster living in the Cathedral Close, who absolutely hates change. Those of us who refuse to accept internet banking will surely appreciate Miss Stanbury's refusal to drop her letters in one of the new-fangled and not-to-be-trusted pillar boxes – the joke being that Trollope had been responsible for introducing the 'letter-receiving pillar' to Britain.

Miss Stanbury is said to have been based on a friend of Trollope's mother, a Miss Fanny Bird who lived in the Cathedral Close. Looking through the Exeter censuses, I have failed to find any elderly lady of that fairly distinctive name, though I did find a Mrs Elizabeth Fanny Bird, wife of an auctioneeer and five years younger than Trollope, in nearby Paris Street. (I also found the cathedral organist, a Mr Alfred Angel, a name which surely should have come from a Victorian novel: he would have been just the man to spar with the nasty Low Church Mr Prong from *Rachel Ray*.) But really, how much do such identifications matter? What the novelist does with those inspirations from people and places is what counts.

Probably Trollope knew Exeter considerably better than he knew Kingsbridge. It is quite possible that his visits to a friend in Exeter, whether his mother's old friend or not, contributed to the cathedral politics of his more famous *Chronicles of Barsetshire*.

Henry Williamson (1895-1977)

The author of *Tarka the Otter* was a Londoner, but he moved to Georgeham, near Croyde, in 1921, when he decided to make writing his career. *Tarka* was published in 1927, and its success meant that Williamson could continue as a full time writer. However in 1936 he bought a farm in Norfolk, where he stayed till his first marriage broke down, returning to Georgeham in 1946, where he produced a novel a year, all now largely forgotten.

Williamson was much affected by his experiences in the First World War, and he wanted to ensure that Britain and Germany would become friends: there must be no more wars. Unfortunately this led him to join the British Union of Fascists. Oswald Mosley became a personal friend, and Williamson thought Hitler was basically a decent man. In 1944 he expressed pleasure when the horrors of the usurious City had been 'relieved a little by the catharsis of high explosive'.

But we should judge an author's work, not the author's personality or politics, and *Tarka the Otter* remains a remarkable book, and not just a children's book. A film was released in 1979. By a macabre coincidence, Williamson apparently died on the same day that the death of Tarka was being filmed.